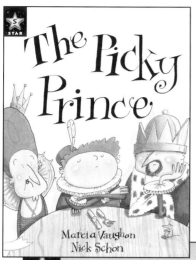

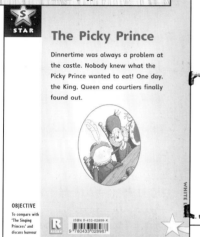

The Picky Prince

Dinnertime was always a problem at the castle. Nobody knew what the Picky Prince wanted to eat! One day, the King, Queen and courtiers finally found out.

OBJECTIVE
To compare with 'The Singing Princess' and discuss humour

ISBN 0-433-02898-X

9 780433 028987

Marcia Vaughan
Illustrated by Nick Schon

The front cover

Why do you think the prince is picky? Have you ever been picky?

What happened?

Where will the story be set?

What other characters are likely to be in the story?

The back cover

Let's read the blurb together. What sort of things do you think the prince will like to eat?

The title page

What does the picture show?

Whose crown do you think it is?

Read the author's and illustrator's names.

Lesson 1 (Chapter 1)

READ

Read pages 2 to 5

Purpose: To find out what happens at dinner.

PAUSE

Pause at page 5

What words tell you that the sun is about to set? (*The sun was sinking like melted cheese over the castle.*)

What do you notice about the way the food is described on page 3? (*alliteration*)

Ask the children to identify any words which they found difficult. What did they do to work them out?

Why do you think the author called the knight 'Sir Rodney Ramcastle'?

Chapter 1

It was a beautiful evening. The sun was sinking like melted cheese over the castle.

The Picky Prince went into the royal dining room. He sat down and looked at the table.

There were silver plates and golden bowls full of different foods.

There were crunchy carrots and buttered beans.

There was freshly baked bread and spicy sausage.

There were fancy fruit muffins, sweet strawberries, and ice cream.

The feast smelled delicious to everyone but the prince!

The prince banged his silver spoon on the table. He sighed heavily.

"I want something special for dinner!" he said. "And it must be *round*!"

"Round, my dear?" said the queen. "Round? Whatever next!"

"Round?" said the king. "Whatever can you want?"

Sir Rodney Ramcastle clanked his armour and said, "Your Majesty, I know *exactly* what the prince wants."

"Then go and get it right away," commanded the king and queen.

READ

Read pages 6 to 8

Purpose: Will the prince be happy with Sir
Rodney's offering?

PAUSE

Pause at page 8

What word describes Sir Rodney walking to the kitchen?
(*clanking*) Do you think knights really wore suits of
armour for dinner?

Why are the crumpets and jam called 'cannonball
crumpets' and 'battering ram jam'? What word-play types
are they using? (*alliteration and rhyme*)

What would you give the prince that is round and gooey?

Why does the prince cry 'phooey!'? What else could the
prince have cried? (*yuck!*)

What words tell you that the sun has set? (*The sun had set
and the sky was as red as tomato sauce.*)

Sir Rodney clanked off to the kitchen and came back with a silver tray.

"What's this?" asked the prince.

"Cannonball crumpets with battering ram jam," clanked Sir Rodney. "Nice and round!"

The prince looked outside. The sun had set and the sky was as red as tomato sauce. Then the prince looked at the cannonball crumpets. He dipped a finger in the battering ram jam and licked it.

"Phooey!" cried the prince. He crossed his eyes and then spat jam all over. "I want something round and *gooey*."

"Round and gooey?" said Sir Rodney. "Well, why didn't you say so?"

READ

Read pages 9 to 11

Purpose: To find out if the Jester of Jolliness can do any better than the knight.

PAUSE

Pause at page 11

What do you think a jester is? (*A person who does funny things to amuse the king and queen.*) What sort of silly things does he do? How do you think he speaks?

Compare the description of the jester on page 10 with the knight on page 6.

How does the author give us a picture of the characters? (*They move and talk in a funny way.*)

'Phooey' is a made-up word for a sound. Can you find another made-up word? (*gooey*)

Please turn to page 15 for Revisit and Respond activities.

"Whatever next!" said the queen.

"Who else can help?"

The Jester of Jolliness jumped for joy and said, "I think I know! I know *exactly* what the prince wants for dinner!"

"Then go and make it right away," commanded the queen and king.

9

The jester cartwheeled off to the kitchen and came back with a big bowl.

"What's this?" asked the prince.

"Jellied eels in banana peels," laughed the jester. "They are round and gooey."

10

The prince looked at the jellied eels in banana peels. They were slithery and slimy and cold. He picked one up and bit into it.

"Phooey!" pouted the prince. He made a face like a rotten apple. "This isn't what I want at all. I want something round and gooey, and *spicy*, too."

The jester wasn't jolly now. "Spicy?" he said. "No, jellied eels aren't spicy."

11

7

Lesson 2 (Chapter 2)

RECAP

Recap lesson 1

What is the prince being picky about?

Who has tried to tempt him with food?

What food did they make?

What does the prince say he wants to eat? (*Something round and gooey, and spicy, too.*)

READ

Read pages 12 to 15

Purpose: To find out who tries to make the prince some food next.

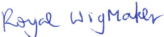
Royal WigMaker

PAUSE

Pause at page 15

Who made some food this time? How does the king feel? (*rather fed up*)

What words describe the Moon on page 12? (*as white as newly baked bread, as round as a slice of salami*)

Find 'commanded' on page 13. What does it mean? What other words mean the same or similar? (*told, ordered, demanded*)

What was wrong with the wig maker's soup? not extra chewy

Find words that describe what the prince wants. (*round, gooey, spicy, extra chewy*)

Chapter 2

Outside, the moon was rising. It was as white as newly baked bread and as round as a slice of salami.

"It will soon be time for the prince to go to bed," said the queen, "and he still hasn't had any dinner!"

The Royal Wig Maker looked up. She fluffed up her sky-high hairdo and said, "I think I know *exactly* what the prince wants."

"Then go and get it, quickly!" commanded the king.

The wig maker went off to the kitchen and came back with a green bowl.

"What's this?" asked the prince.

"Hot hair-net soup," said the wig maker. "The bowl is round and the soup is gooey and spicy!"

The prince looked at the soup. He dipped the ladle in and took a sip.

"Phooey!" cried the prince. He gulped down a glass of water. "That won't do at all! I want something round and gooey and spicy and extra *chewy*."

"Hot hair-net soup is spicy," said the wig maker. "But it isn't chewy. No, it isn't chewy at all," and she shook her head.

READ

Read pages 16 to 19

Purpose: To find out who knows what exactly the prince wants to eat for his dinner.

PAUSE

Pause at page 19

What does the prince decide to do?

Where does the prince go?

Ask the children to read 'I know *exactly* what…' (page 17). Ask them to explain '*exactly*'.

The queen sighed and the king put his head in his hands. Who could help them now?

The prince looked at them and said, "There is only *one* person in the whole castle who knows what I want to eat for dinner."

Then everyone asked, "Who? Who can it be?"

"Who do you think?" said the prince. "That person is . . . *me*! I know *exactly* what I want for dinner."

"Hurrah! We'll make it for you right away," said everyone.

"No," said the prince. "I can make it all by myself."

The prince pushed back his chair, and marched past the queen, the king, the knight, the jester and the wig maker. He walked all the way through the castle until he came to the royal kitchen.

11

Read pages 20 to 21

Purpose: To find out what the prince does in the kitchen.

Pause at page 21

What ingredients does he get in the kitchen?

What is round? (*dough*)
What is gooey? (*tomato sauce*)
What is spicy? (*salami*)
What is extra chewy? (*cheese*)

What words tell you the salami is big? (*the size of an elephant's trunk*)

What do you think he is making?

Read pages 22 to the end

Purpose: To find out what the prince cooks.

The prince got out a bowl of dough,
a bucket of tomato sauce, a wheel of cheese,
and a salami the size of an elephant's trunk.
Then the Picky Prince rolled up his ruffled
sleeves and went to work.

"What is the prince cooking?" wondered
the queen and king.

"I don't know," said Sir Rodney Ramcastle.
"But it's bound to be round!"

"And it's got to be gooey!" said the Jester
of Jolliness.

"And it's sure to be spicy!" said the Royal
Wig Maker.

"This," said the prince, "is my favourite
thing to eat in the whole wide world."

Suddenly, a delicious smell filled the kitchen.
Noses twitched. Tastebuds itched.

Everyone crowded around the prince as
he opened the oven door and pulled out
his dinner.

"It's *so* round!" declared Sir Rodney.

"It's *so* gooey!" exclaimed the jester.

"It smells *so* spicy!" sniffed the wig maker.

"Whatever can it be?" wondered the
queen and king.

"It's . . . pizza!" said the prince, "and I made
enough for everyone in the castle!"

"Delicious!" grinned the queen.

"Delicious!" laughed the king.

"Hurrah!" cheered the rest of the royal court.

But the prince did not say a word, because his mouth was full of round, gooey, spicy, chewy pizza!

24

PAUSE

Pause at page 24

What is the prince's favourite food?

What does 'Delicious' mean? What other words could be used instead?

After Reading

Revisit and Respond

Lesson 1

T What would you give the prince to eat? If you were being picky, what would you want to eat?

T Ask the children to make a list of the phrases, words and events in the story that they find funny.

T Make up another character who could make a dish for the prince. What name would you have for the dish? Make up some funny rhyming foods.

W Go through the text and find examples of word play, e.g. rhyme or alliteration.

Lesson 2

T Ask the children to read the descriptions of the sun, sky and moon on pages 2, 7 and 12. Do they notice anything about the foods used to describe the sun, the moon and the sky? Are they clues about what the prince wants to eat? (*cheese, tomato, bread, salami – they are the ingredients of pizza*)

T Look at the words used to describe the pizza. Classify them into words to do with shape, texture and taste. Ask the children to think of a favourite food and describe it to the rest of the group in terms of shape, texture and colour.

T Remind the children of another story at Rigby Star White Level, *The Singing Princess*. Ask them in groups to think of the similarities between the two stories. (E.g. *both funny; neither fit the fairy tale image of handsome prince and beautiful princess; both have 'unprincely' problems: fussy eating, raucous singing voice; and both main characters are bossy.*)

W Ask the children to look for phrases that describe things (i.e. analogies like *a salami the size of an elephant's trunk*). Ask them to make up their own funny ways to describe types of food (*e.g. custard as lumpy as quicksand*), and write them down. Discuss what they come up with.

W Play 'I am thinking' with the children. Choose a word from the story and give the children the page number. Say 'I am thinking of a word … (and give a description). E.g. (page 22) 'I am thinking of a word that has 'ed' at the end and means moved a little bit' (*twitched*).